D1060756

WEEKLY **WR** READER®
EARLY LEARNING LIBRARY

Raccoons

Are Night Animals

by Joanne Mattern

Reading consultant: Susan Nations, M.Ed., author/literacy coach/consultant in literacy development
Science and curriculum consultant: Debra Voege, M.A., science and math curriculum resource teacher

Please visit our web site at: www.garethstevens.com
For a free color catalog describing Weekly Reader® Early Learning Library's list
of high-quality books, call 1-877-445-5824 (USA) or 1-800-387-3178 (Canada).
Weekly Reader® Early Learning Library's fax: (414) 336-0164.

Library of Congress Cataloging-in-Publication Data

Mattern, Joanne, 1963-
    Raccoons are night animals / by Joanne Mattern.
        p. cm. — (Night animals)
    Includes bibliographical references and index.
    ISBN-13: 978-0-8368-7849-3 (lib. bdg.)
    ISBN-13: 978-0-8368-7856-1 (softcover)
    1. Raccoons—Juvenile literature.   I. Title.
    QL737.C26M38   2007
    599.76'32—dc22   2006030885

This edition first published in 2007 by
Weekly Reader® Early Learning Library
A Member of the WRC Media Family of Companies
330 West Olive Street, Suite 100
Milwaukee, Wisconsin 53212 USA

Editor: Tea Benduhn
Art direction: Tammy West
Cover design and page layout: Scott M. Krall
Picture research: Diane Laska-Swanke

Picture credits: Cover, title page © Craig K. Lorenz/Photo Researchers, Inc.; p. 5 © Michael Durham/Visuals Unlimited;
p. 7 © Steve Maslowski/Visuals Unlimited; p. 9 © Medford Taylor/National Geographic Image Collection;
p. 11 © Jeanne White/Photo Researchers, Inc.; p. 13 © Stephen J. Krasemann/Photo Researchers, Inc.;
p. 15 © Thomas Kitchin & Victoria Hurst/leesonphoto; p. 17 © Michael Durham/naturepl.com;
p. 19 © Tom J. Ulrich/Visuals Unlimited; p. 21 © Stephen St. John/National Geographic Image Collection

Printed in the United States of America

1 2 3 4 5 6 7 8 9 10 10 09 08 07 06

Note to Educators and Parents

Reading is such an exciting adventure for young children! They are beginning to integrate their oral language skills with written language. To encourage children along the path to early literacy, books must be colorful, engaging, and interesting; they should invite the young reader to explore both the print and the pictures.

The *Night Animals* series is designed to help children read about creatures that are active during the night. Each book explains what a different night animal does during the day, how it finds food, and how it adapts to its nocturnal life.

Each book is specially designed to support the young reader in the reading process. The familiar topics are appealing to young children and invite them to read — and reread — again and again. The full-color photographs and enhanced text further support the student during the reading process.

In addition to serving as wonderful picture books in schools, libraries, homes, and other places where children learn to love reading, these books are specifically intended to be read within an instructional guided reading group. This small group setting allows beginning readers to work with a fluent adult model as they make meaning from the text. After children develop fluency with the text and content, the books can be read independently. Children and adults alike will find these books supportive, engaging, and fun!

— Susan Nations, M.Ed., author/literacy coach/
consultant in literacy development

Is that a **masked bandit**?

No. It is a raccoon!

Raccoons are very active at night. During the day, most raccoons sleep. A hollow log is a safe place for raccoons to sleep!

Raccoons come out at night to look for food. They can see well in the dark. Their good **eyesight** helps them find their way around.

A raccoon also uses its sharp **sense** of smell to find its way around and to look for food.

Raccoons find food near their homes. Some live in the country or in woods. Others live in backyards or city parks.

Raccoons have special front **paws** that look like hands. They can hold food in their paws.

In the city, they can use their paws to open garbage cans. Sometimes, they search through garbage to find a meal.

A raccoon often dips its food in water before it eats. It looks like it is washing its food! Water helps the raccoon feel the parts of food it does not want to eat.

Raccoons find many ways to eat. They are **clever** night animals.

Glossary

bandit — someone who steals things

clever — good at figuring out puzzles

eyesight — the ability to see

garbage — trash, scraps of food, or used things that people throw away

hollow — empty inside

masked — wearing a covering over the eyes or over the whole face

paws — an animal's feet

sense — one of an animal's abilities, such as seeing, hearing, smelling, tasting, or feeling

For More Information

Books

Clever Raccoons. Pull Ahead Books (series). Kristin L. Nelson (Lerner Publications)

Raccoons. William John Ripple (Pebble Books)

Raccoons. Early Bird Nature Books (series). L. Patricia Kite (Lerner Publications)

Raccoons. Rookie Read-About Science (series). Allan Fowler (Children's Press)

Web Site

Environmental Education for Kids! Raccoon
www.dnr.state.wi.us/org/caer/ce/eek/critter/mammal/ raccoon.htm
This site has lots of fun facts about these backyard "bandits."

Publisher's note to educators and parents: Our editors have carefully reviewed this Web site to ensure that it is suitable for children. Many Web sites change frequently, however, and we cannot guarantee that a site's future contents will continue to meet our high standards of quality and educational value. Be advised that children should be closely supervised whenever they access the Internet.

Index

About the Author

Joanne Mattern has written more than 150 books for children. She has written about unusual animals, sports, history, world cities, and many other topics. Joanne also works in her local library. She lives in New York State with her husband, three daughters, and assorted pets. She enjoys animals, music, reading, going to baseball games, and visiting schools to talk about her books.